Art Media Series

Creating with Found Objects

Lothar Kampmann

 Van Nostrand Reinhold Company/New York

Illustrations
The illustrations in the first part of the book are by students of the Ruhr Teachers' Training College, Dortmund Section, and by the author. The illustrations in the Appendix are from the archives of the Department of Art and Craft Education of the Ruhr Teachers' Training College, Dortmund Section. A further source was the Overberg School, Recklinghausen.

Photographs: Wilhelm Homann, Recklinghausen (69); Prestel Verlag, Munich (1); Städtische Kunsthalle, Mannheim (1).

Sponsored by the Günther Wagner Pelikan-Werke, Hanover; and Koh-I-Nor, Inc., 100 North Street, Bergen, New Jersey 08804.

German edition © 1971 by Otto Maier Verlag, Ravensburg, Germany.

English translation Copyright ©1973 by Evans Brothers Limited.

Library of Congress Catalog Card Number 72–2792
ISBN 0–442–24249–2

Printed in Italy

Published in the United States of America, 1973, by Van Nostrand Reinhold Company, a Division of Litton Educational Publishing, Inc., 450 West 33rd Street, New York, N.Y. 10001.

16 15 14 13 12 11 10 9 8 7 6 5 4 3 2 1

Introduction

When we were children our pockets were usually full of all sorts of things which we had simply picked up as we went along. They meant a great deal to us and we guarded them like treasures, seeing and using them in our own particular way.

No doubt we came across most of these things totally by accident. Others were perhaps found by looking, though even these were in a sense picked up by chance in so far as we were not consciously aware of looking for anything specific. And we had a use for all these things, which is, of course, the key to the secret of stuffed pockets. As adults we have lost this key for the simple reason that we see everything in terms of raw materials and end products; everything must have a deeper meaning or an economic purpose.

Children have the ability to pretend. To them a matchbox can become a house, a pencil can be a rocket, and so on. In this way they are able to make contact with objects and use them. Objects become important to them and they feel an allegiance towards the things they find. Unfortunately the adult's interest usually dies with his assessment of an object's practical usefulness; he categorizes the object and quickly forgets it.

Their natural curiosity leads children to take an interest in everything that goes on in the world. They have a spontaneous conception of the many different uses to which an object can be put; they know that any object is capable of being 'transformed'.

The adult, however, does not see things in the same way; the things which he picks up by chance are usually only interesting in so far as they are rare or unusual.

In order to be able to find things, we need the ability to see in the fullest sense of the word; merely to perceive the world optically is not enough. We have to immerse

3

ourselves in the visual variety which the world offers us. In this way we can truly appreciate objects and gain insight into their essence and all their possible functions. Our sense of touch is also important to this end, for a sensitive hand helps us to 'see' more clearly.

The eye registers objects visually; the hand feels them and either confirms or corrects what the eye has registered; the mind arranges these things, drawing attention to similarities and bringing together different banks of knowledge. We then go on to attach value and emotion to the objects which have been registered. In simple terms this whole process is one of 'seeing'.

In this book we are concerned with more than just seeing, however; in the case of objects found, the visual process must lead on to a desire and willingness to pick the particular object up and do something thoughtful and active with it. Thus the things which we pick up by chance challenge us to be creative—to make something out of them. When we begin to use them creatively, these chance objects come to life; otherwise they simply 'exist' and, when this is the case, the magical powers of chance have been squandered.

It often happens that something which cannot be achieved by sheer hard work suddenly comes about fortuitously and unintentionally. Success might even result from error or carelessness. This is caused by the routine course of events—such as our well-trained sequences of action—being disrupted in some way, bringing about an unexpected, accidental conclusion. One must always be receptive to this sort of chance occurrence in order never to miss the opportunity of experiencing something new.

But what is 'chance'? In a way it is like a game of dice; no one knows which numbers will turn up, and chance allows the dice to roll as they wish. We can benefit from this state of affairs by making creative use of everyday objects and adopting 'aleatory techniques'. (Aleatory—from the Latin *alea* (die)—means, strictly speaking, 'depending on the throw of a die', and we have bluntly transferred the meaning to 'by chance'.)

Everyday objects and things picked up by chance are intrinsically valuable and alive; they are capable of all sorts of pictorial transformation so long as we progress from seeing them in a purely practical, material light and develop a creative interest in them.

Jackson Pollock at work. From *Schule des Schauens* by Max Burchartz, by kind permission of Prestel Verlag, Munich.

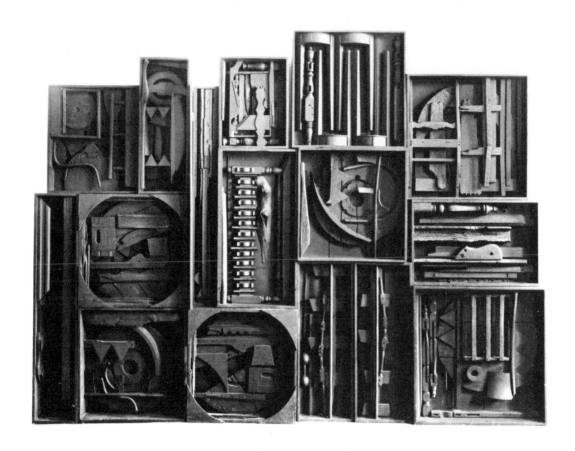

Louise Nevelson: Vision one, 1961.
A wall made of 15 black wooden
boxes, 9 ft high, 13 ft wide.
Städtische Kunsthalle, Mannheim.

Chance and object

In the context of this book, dealing with chance and objects is not confined merely to finding, recognizing and collecting. There is more to it than that. The chance find forms an inducement; it is simply a starting point. Our work with it is not 'chancey', but is a conscious application. The chance element is always present when we deal with any sort of material, and we consciously provoke this.

We 'invent' new contingencies and try to find out how the chance aspect came about. We experiment with chance and by experimenting we transform the known quantity, investigate new aspects of it, and search for further 'possible impossibilities'.

We examine the chance find to see whether it could lend itself to new uses. These may be alien to its actual purpose, but may be possible because of the object's shape, colour, substance or function.

We give conscious directions to chance occurrences. We change them around to fit our own pictorial needs. We take away the object's innate function and, by replacing it with something new, lend it new expression as a pictorial object. In this way chance finds become material for new sorts of pictorial objects. We transform the object or invent a new one.

Invention and transformation belong to man's primitive creative abilities. Everyone possesses the ability to be creative; it is just that some people have more impulsive energy than others. Whenever interest is aroused, the impulse to be 'creative' with the particular object exists. But all too often one lacks the ability to consider things at length and in a leisurely manner, and therefore to realize one's impulses.

When this is the case, one sees chance simply as an error; one only recognizes the object's original purpose, and then one's view is obstructed. So if clumsy hands and eyes are now combined with clumsy thinking, even the greatest natural ability will achieve nothing. But if one experiments with the object and deals with it in a spirit of curiosity, one's hands, eyes and brain are given the opportunity to be dextrous.

The aim of this book is to inspire the wish to deal with and transform objects and materials. It attempts to show parents and teachers where to look for and find points of application; these will then prove to be greater and more varied than it is possible to cover in the space available here. But the illustrations will, it is hoped, provide the stimulus to look for new sources of chance finds and to come across new objects—things which previously seemed useless, but which can become aesthetic objects if used creatively.

Chance
We are not concerned here with the *methods* of chance and objects; for chance has no method.

Children face chance with less reservations than adults. They meet it mainly while playing. In the life of the child, playing with materials represents an inquiring experiment offering the opportunity of insight. These insights are not gained by any form of work; they simply come to the child during play.

Here is an example of such 'play'. Mother is peeling apples; if she does not want the peel, it can form an ideal material for a chance-game. It is important that the peel should be in the form of a long,

narrow strip, almost like a coil. If you just drop the peel on the floor, it will adopt a shape. Looking at this shape, you can interpret it in any way you like.

The pouring of molten lead into water is a similar example. Chance is also involved here, but it can be manipulated as in the game with apple peel. The peel can be thrown or simply dropped; or it can be placed on the floor according to one's own exact wishes. In the same way hot, molten lead can be poured slowly, quickly, gently or forcefully into water. Whether the water is hot, cold or icy also makes a lot of difference.

These two chance games form a starting point for dealing and experimenting with objects.

What does the apple peel game consist of? A long strip—like a piece of string—falls to the floor and 'draws' a shape.

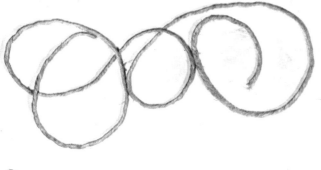

Now take a real piece of string—or a thick piece of cord—and drop it on the floor. Each time you drop it, it will take on a different shape. While doing this you suddenly realize that you do not 'like' every shape. Our eyes register 'aesthetic correctness'; that is, the mysterious and yet perfect manner of correlation and lineation, which may strike us as bewildering, peaceful or harmonious, or may remind us of 'this or that'. These will be fleeting and ever-changing shapes.

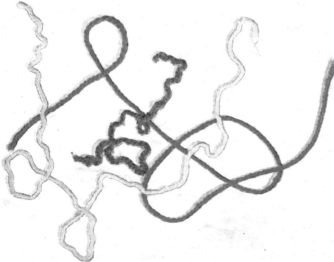

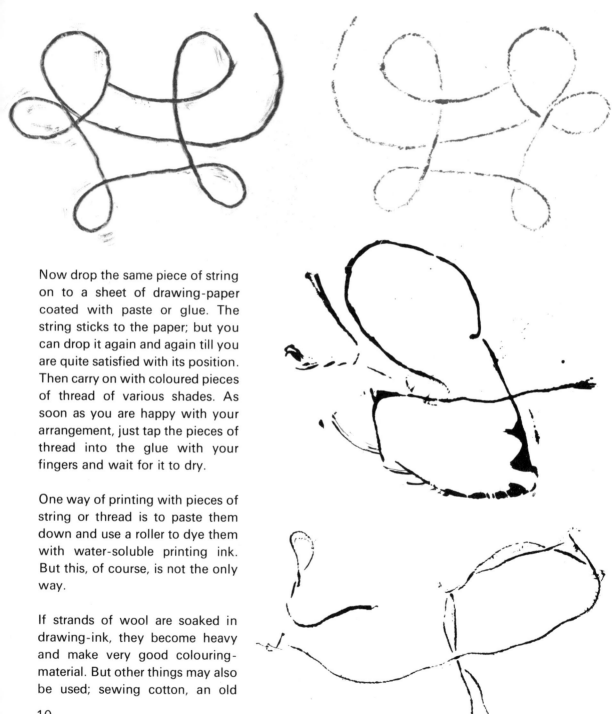

Now drop the same piece of string on to a sheet of drawing-paper coated with paste or glue. The string sticks to the paper; but you can drop it again and again till you are quite satisfied with its position. Then carry on with coloured pieces of thread of various shades. As soon as you are happy with your arrangement, just tap the pieces of thread into the glue with your fingers and wait for it to dry.

One way of printing with pieces of string or thread is to paste them down and use a roller to dye them with water-soluble printing ink. But this, of course, is not the only way.

If strands of wool are soaked in drawing-ink, they become heavy and make very good colouring-material. But other things may also be used; sewing cotton, an old

curtain cord, packing string or a rubber band will do equally well. All these things, if soaked in ink or runny paint, leave their own special kind of random colour traces when they are dropped on to paper. One can also place the string or other material on to the piece of paper, then press a second piece of paper on top of it, and change the position of the string with the latter.

It is also possible to do exactly the same by using some general-purpose adhesive. Once the first drop has been squeezed out of the tube, the adhesive comes pouring out in the form of a long string—as if controlled by an invisible hand. If you drip the adhesive on to a glass plate and allow it to dry, you can then dye the relief with an inking roller and use the plate as a block. Acrylic, formica and other plastic materials can also be used as a base. If you use cardboard or other types of absorbent material, however, the adhesive will sink in and this will affect the relief. The random traces obtained tempt one into looking for new shapes and discovering new figures.

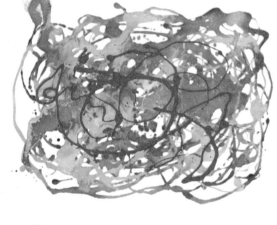

Let us now develop this idea of dropping things on to various bases even further. When eating treacle or honey with bread, children like to hold the spoon up and let the treacle or honey drip down on to the bread.

We can use this idea by simply replacing the treacle with coloured enamel and using it to 'paint' a piece of cardboard or stiff drawing paper. But certain things have to be considered. How runny should the enamel be? Does it react differently to absorbent and non-absorbent surfaces?

At the first attempt you will find it difficult to control the dripping enamel; it may run out in drops rather than threads. It may run all over the place just when you are quite happy with the result.

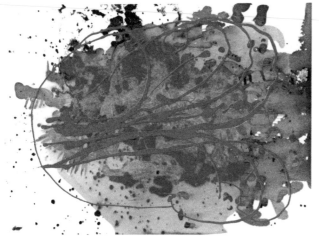

During the following experiments we shall make use of what we have learnt in our previous attempts. It is possible that we do not know how and where to place the drops and threads, and how to incorporate the places where the paint has run. We are now in a position consciously to exploit chance and use it for our own pictorial expression.

Drops of viscous material fall in a different way from drops of runny liquids such as drawing ink or water colour. They do not produce threads, but burst at the moment of impact with the base. They therefore make new surface formations possible.

If you drip drawing ink on to a wet surface, you will produce sun-like blobs which run into each other. The ink forms a 'floating' film on top of the water.

13

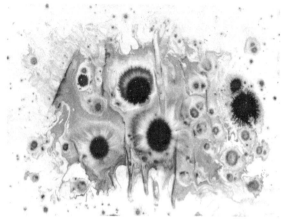

If you hold the paper at a sloping angle or almost vertical and then drip the ink on to it, you will find that elongated shapes—running downwards—are formed. These can now be used to make new combinations if the flow of ink is suddenly disrupted by a change in the position of the paper, so that some drops meet the paper at an angle and others meet it straight on.

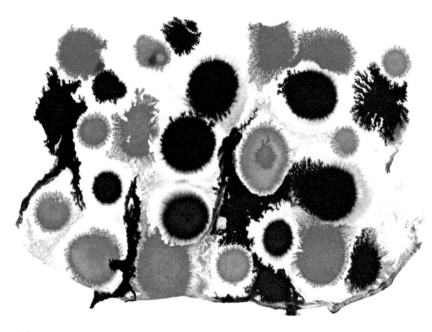

Even a simple drop falling on to a tilted sheet of dry paper can be graphically very attractive. The single drops just need to be well arranged.

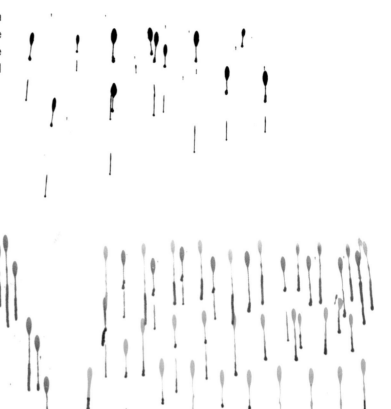

You may quite often find, however, that the consistency of the ink is not quite right, and the drops may run down the paper. But this can also be used with advantage; the drops will leave tracks which can easily be guided by turning the paper.

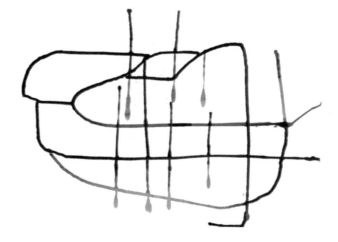

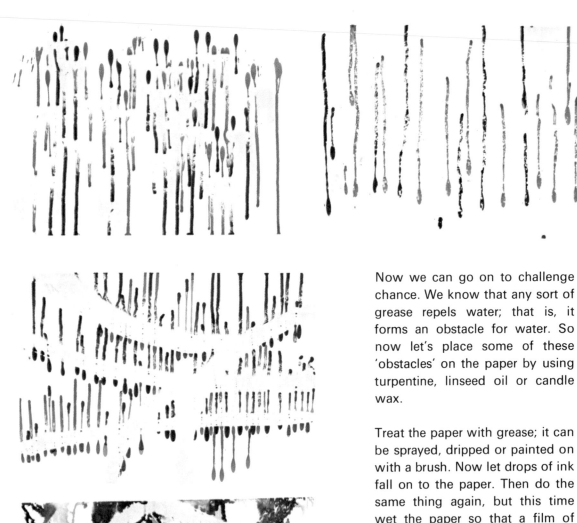

Now we can go on to challenge chance. We know that any sort of grease repels water; that is, it forms an obstacle for water. So now let's place some of these 'obstacles' on the paper by using turpentine, linseed oil or candle wax.

Treat the paper with grease; it can be sprayed, dripped or painted on with a brush. Now let drops of ink fall on to the paper. Then do the same thing again, but this time wet the paper so that a film of water forms on top of it. By these methods the flow of ink will be disrupted.

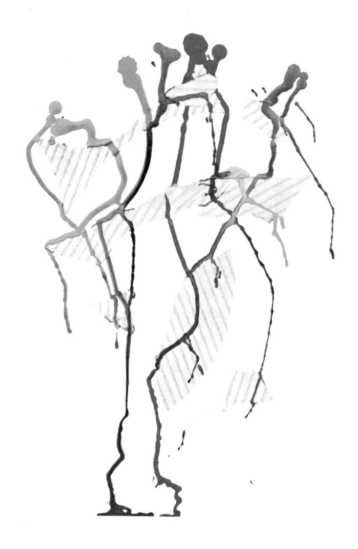

Another way of obstructing the course of the drops is by sticking additional scraps of paper of various sizes to the sheet.

Chance takes its own course according to its own inherent laws. If one studies them, one comes to realize that these laws are self-evident. One has only to study them in order to know how to apply them. Once we know how the chance occurrence came about, we can consciously repeat it. Then whatever we do can be regarded as a genuine experiment.

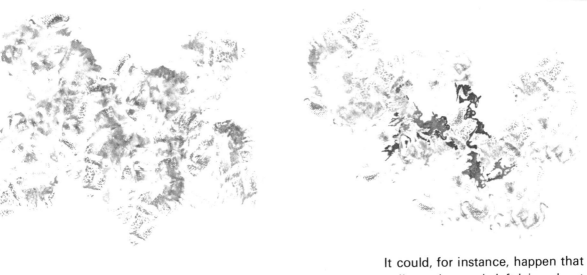

It could, for instance, happen that a dirty paint-rag is left lying about on the table, and quite by chance you happen to place a clean printing sheet right on top of it. The result is a chance print, which could in future be reproduced consciously.

By studying such 'random pictorial objects' carefully one realizes that they have a special charm. They are structured in so interesting a way that one begins to wonder if it is at all possible to produce such patterns from different materials. And one comes to the conclusion that it would indeed be difficult, perhaps even impossible. But there are ways; a crumpled or folded sheet of paper dyed with a roller and then printed, for example. Developing this further, one can go on to experiment with various other materials. The printed result will always come about 'by chance'. But many different aspects will play an important part: when crumpled or folded, some materials form fine creases, whereas others form rough, uneven creases; some materials have a fine texture; others a coarse texture; different inks and paints do not stick to the material equally well; paint which is beginning to dry creates a different print from wet paint. One can only find these things out by experimenting.

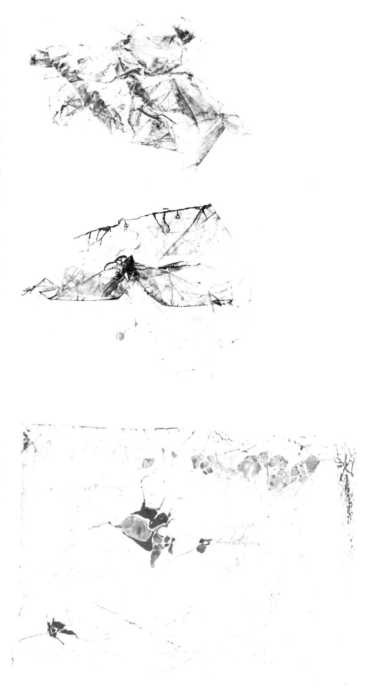

Making random objects into pictures

What do we do with the random objects which we come across? We test them to see if they can be 'used' in some way, if they could 'lead on' to something, if we can 'make something out of' them. For things which arise or are found by chance have no artistic or creative value of their own. They have only a greater or lesser aesthetic value; and to track this down is a pictorial problem.

It should be our aim to reproduce and transform these aesthetic objects, which are simply pictorial phenomena presented to us by chance. They should encourage us to be active in a pictorial way. Just as a novel, interesting or surprising association of ideas motivates our thoughts, so should these chance occurrences form pictorial motivation. On the following pages objects or parts of objects are transformed by pictorial or graphic means, as was the case with some of the examples already shown. They could, of course, just as well have been treated in various other ways.

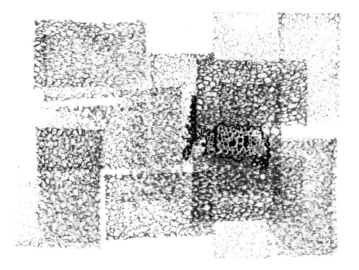

Impression from a sponge.

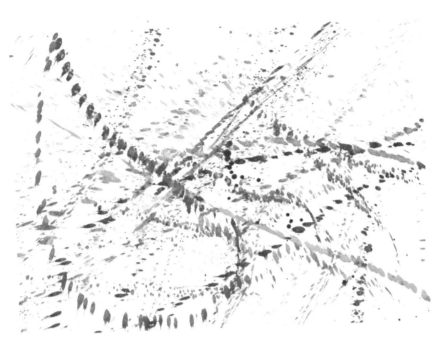

Splashes of paint—made by flick-
ing the brush—on white or
coloured paper.

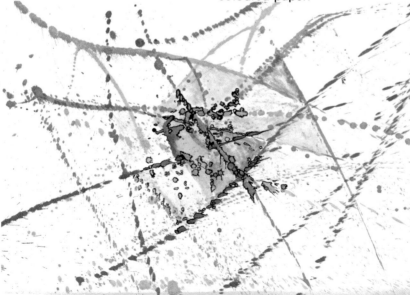

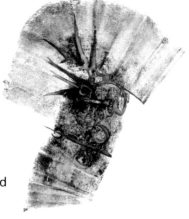

Paper on which a roller was rolled clean.

Crumpled wet paper covered with paint. The engraving-like quality was achieved by rubbing a black wax crayon (lengthways) over the paper when the paint had dried.

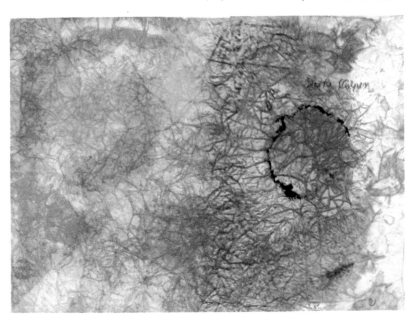

Paper that was placed on a table smeared with paint and then removed.

Rubbing from a wooden plank. Drawing paper was placed on the plank and rubbed with wax crayons.

24

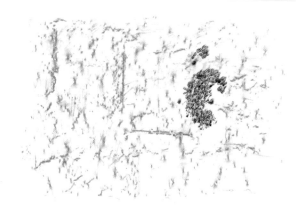

Rubbing from an unplastered wall. (A rubbing can be made from coarse linen, ornamental glass, grating, wire mesh, floorboards, rush-matting, etc.)

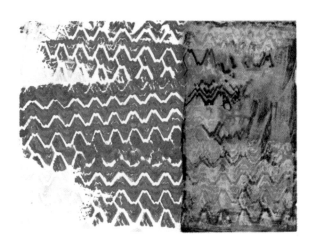

Tyre marks.

Paper pressed on leaves sprayed with paint.

Paper painted with distemper, pressed on a spray of leaves and then removed.

A sheet of paper was burnt, and then drawing paper coated with paste was placed on top of it.

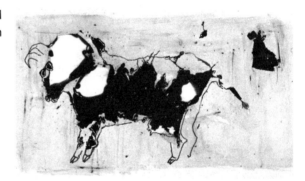

A round log dyed and rolled on paper.

Ink was placed between two glass plates, which were then separated and pressed on to paper.

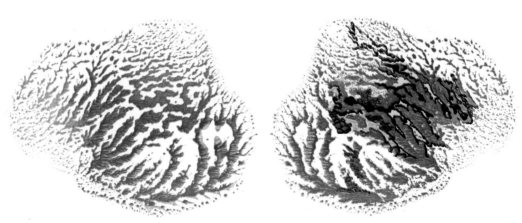

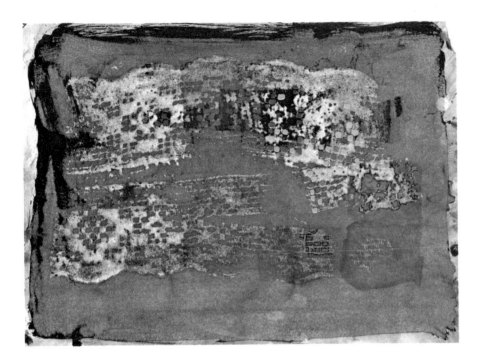

Coarse pieces of material were soaked in clear varnish and pressed on to paper. The impression of the material left on the paper repelled water, water colour and ink.

All these 'pictures' were created consciously. Chance was challenged. But each example could have been produced purely by chance, and however much conscious thought went into their creation, it was impossible to tell in advance what the result would look like.

But the creation of chance-objects is not limited to surface; they can also be three-dimensional.

If someone pressed his fingers into a slab of clay which you had carefully moulded, you might think that it was ruined. But why destroy this chance product?

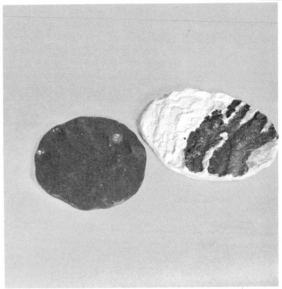

You could easily wait for the clay to dry and carry on from the chance occurrence by making incisions or scratch lines. Or you could leave it exactly as it is and, when it is dry, fire and glaze it. You could also paint it—with casein emulsion, for example—and coat it with clear varnish.

There are many ways in which three-dimensional chance-products may be created. They are another sort of 'pictorial gift' and lend themselves to all types of transformation.

1

A slab of soft clay is beaten with birch rods—either at random or according to a set plan.

2

A slab of soft clay is handled a number of times and pressed with the fingers. Strange jagged bumps are produced.

3

Stems and flowers are pressed into a slab of soft clay. The slab is allowed to dry and then fired. The stems, leaves and flowers form negative moulds. They can be painted and glazed.

4

A slab of soft clay is pressed against the bark of a tree and allowed to dry. The pattern of the bark is left on the clay. This is a counterpart of rubbing (see page 25).

5

A slab of soft clay is pressed into a lawn. Everything that happens to be there—grass, weeds, small stones, etc.—will be recorded.

6

Smaller and larger pieces of clay are thrown with great force against a slab of soft clay. The lumps will stick to the surface and dry as part of the structure.

7

Pieces of polystyrene of various sizes are pressed into a slab of soft clay. When it has been allowed to dry, the slab is fired. The polystyrene burns and leaves holes in the clay.

30

8

A heap of fine grain sand is sprinkled with water from a small watering can.

a Plaster of Paris is poured over it and then removed when it has hardened. The cast is rinsed out with water.

b It is fixed by spraying it a few times with a mixture of adhesive and water. After a day or two the sand will have dried and the adhesive layer (a strong sandy crust) can be lifted off and washed out with water.

Chance, experiment, object, further development; all these things overlap. One springs from the other.

However carefully one pours the water, the patterns made in the sand will always depend on chance. Only now can the creative pictorial work begin. The person who finds one of chance's more beautiful creations hardly has the right to think that he has produced something artistic. But he can be proud of his artistic eye, and he should have the artistic ability to make something out of this chance find.

Chance is a strange thing; it is impossible to define it clearly. On the one hand something happens without our knowledge; the result is accidental; but only the first time; from then on we are able to reproduce the result consciously and intentionally. On the other hand, a finished object comes into our hands by chance and we start to think how we could make 'pictorial-optical objects' out of it. And then again there is 'technical chance'; for example, when something goes wrong during a piece of work and causes interesting things to happen—so interesting that it would be a pity not to use them. We place the realization afforded by such an experience amongst our bank of technical knowledge.

One is trying to draw an extremely fine line when the pen suddenly splutters and blotches the paper:

31

sometimes it is only at this point that the drawing becomes interesting.

Or we can paint 'wet on wet'. We might try to depict something that we know well—flowers, fish or houses, for example. When all the colours run into each other, we might think that the painting has been spoilt, but if one is both curious and inventive, one realizes that nothing has gone wrong. On the contrary, a technique which so far has only been a means to an end has proved its intrinsic pictorial value.

The same applies to the well-known method of drawing in ink on wet paper. We must simply look at established methods from a different perspective.

We have already discussed the methods of dripping coloured enamel on to paper or other materials. Now we can go on from this by rubbing the paper with a stick or the end of a paint brush, which will produce a streaky effect. One could make a print of this on another sheet of paper, and complete the picture by painting it over with turpentine or some other solution.

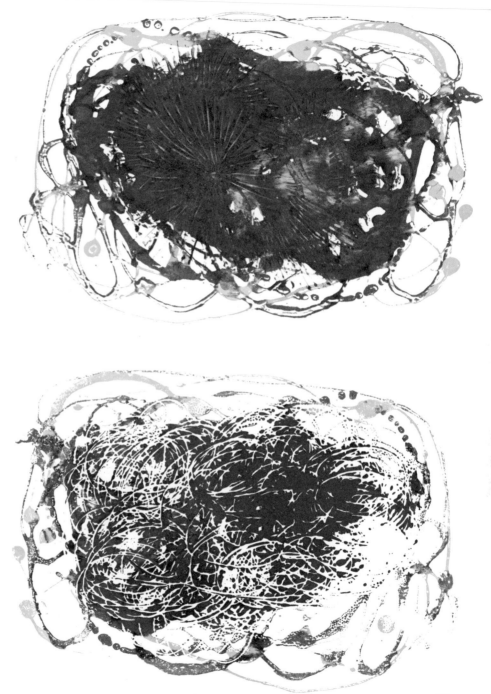

We can make use of the fact that turpentine dissolves enamels. They will turn into colourful oily liquids; and oil floats on water. When you have dissolved the enamels with turpentine or some other appropriate solution, pour them over the wet surface. The colours will run into each other. Mix them up with a stick. If you now place a sheet of paper on this multicoloured surface, it will soak up the enamel solution. So this is yet another way of printing. And again there is room for experiment. Oil paints will react differently from enamels when dissolved in turpentine. These different conditions greatly affect the optical result.

There is, of course, an infinite variety of chance occurrences, and it is inevitable that a great deal has been left out in this summary. At least this allows the reader the opportunity to outdo the author.

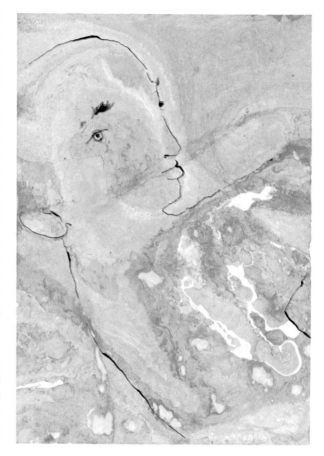

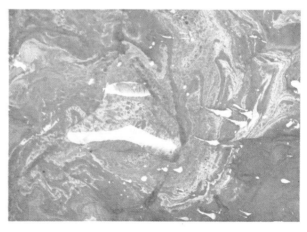

Objects, discoveries and environment

So long as we do not curb our creative tendencies, we are able to look upon the everyday objects which we come across and pick up as things to be used pictorially. We see that it is possible to transform or 'manipulate' them to meet our own particular aesthetic wishes.

The question is, where are these objects, what do they look like, and how are we to 'manipulate' them? The answer is simple. All things which are lying around are objects; they are there waiting for us to transform them into meaningful pictures.

But what is meaningful? Anything which engages a child's attention and activity is meaningful. Small children sit on a terrace with a pebble floor and, with great excitement and concentration, paint the pebbles with clear water. It satisfies them to make dull, dry stones wet and shiny. Or they quite happily paint the fence with water. In both cases they are playing, while at the same time dealing with and transforming materials.

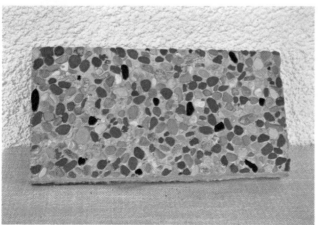

The step from a playful to a pictorial pursuit is a small one. For example:

a We let the children have poster paints instead of water. They may paint each individual stone a different colour if they wish.
b They embellish the surface.
c They make shapes and figures on the surface and get to know the beauty of a mosaic.

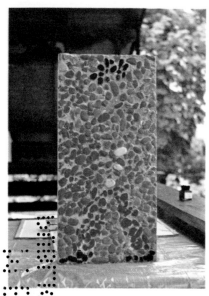

If we can paint a 'mosaic', we might just as well go out and look for brightly-coloured stones in order to make our own mosaic. The placing and arranging of the stones is of greatest importance. The best way of doing this is by using a piece of modelling clay as a base. The stones will then stick easily, but can also be moved about at will.

There are many methods of making such mosaics permanent. Three of these methods may be carried out without any great technical difficulty. It is advisable to use a strong piece of wood as a base.

1. Press the stones into putty. When the putty dries off it is completely hard and solid.

2. Set the stones in a filling material such as plaster of Paris.
3. Press the stones into a mixture of three parts fine sand to one part cement.

Pebbles found in the road, near the river, at the beach, in a gravel pit, or on a building site all make excellent objects for pictorial transformation. The simplest thing to do is to paint them. For best results use either casein emulsion or poster paints.

Small children will certainly enjoy splashing the stones with as many colours as possible. The older ones could make use of certain colour combinations: blue and red only; red and green; earth colours combined with black and white; black and white on a bright background; different shades of the same colour. It is quite difficult to paint the pebbles according to their own particular shape.

Pebbles can also be treated graphically—with drawing ink and a steel pen, for example. If you want the drawing to last, it is advisable to coat it with clear varnish. In fact, there are lots of ways in which clear varnish may be used.

Take a limestone or marble pebble and paint a design on it carefully with clear varnish or diluted adhesive. When it has dried, put the stone in black or coloured drawing ink for a short time. Then wipe it clean with a damp cloth. The parts of the stone which had been treated with varnish or adhesive will not have been dyed by the ink.

Just an ordinary stone, but offering a wealth of pictorial possibilities. Let us look at pebbles once more before we move on to something else. This experiment should be done only under the supervision of an adult. Coat a marble pebble with liquid beeswax or stopping-out varnish. Use a brush to do this. Now dip the stone in hydrochloric acid. The acid will eat into the marble, causing cavities and indentations. But be very careful, acid also attacks fingers and clothes.

flat and not particularly unique. Or is it?

There are so many objects which lend themselves to pictorial transformation. It doesn't necessarily have to be a stone which you happen to find on your way home. After all, a pebble is simply round,

We can also use twigs and roots from the woods; these can be transformed by polishing them with sandpaper or by painting them.

If you stick several of these creations together skilfully, you can obtain interesting three-dimensional compositions. The separate elements can be painted either before or after applying the adhesive.

And what can be done with twigs and roots can also be done with pebbles.

What we have only 'stuck together' up till now can be constructed even more effectively by using 'cement', which will also fill in the joints. This is easy to make: just mix some fine sand with adhesive. Such a mixture remains workable for some time. With this cement you can now fill in all the joints in the construction, which before were only put together and strengthened with adhesive.

Now we can move on to larger objects. We can colour and treat these in whatever way we wish. It all looks very easy, but take your time; a great deal of patience is needed!

We can also do exactly the same with small pieces or blocks of wood, such as the waste shavings found in a carpenter's shop. The only difference is that in this case the cement should be made of sawdust and adhesive.

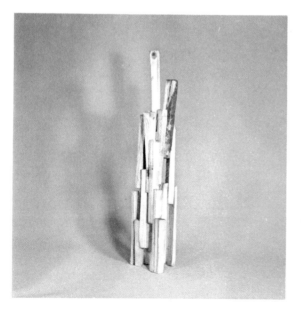

Just think of all the waste material produced by industry: boxes, tins, cans, containers. We should see this as a rich source of creative activity.

With a little bit of imagination they can easily be made into such things as trains, cars, houses and model towns. But this sort of thing quickly becomes a cliché and, while accepting that the world is governed by utility, we should avoid programming our children into this way of thinking. They should be free to build whatever they want to with this scrap material—just as if it were a box of bricks. Whatever is possible is also useful, but not everything is possible. If something is not static, it will collapse.

There is more to it than just building things with these objects. The basic intention must be to transform them; to remove them from their original intended purpose and to give them a new pictorial purpose. All sorts of small boxes, for example, can be turned into a number of things. We have already mentioned that they can be stuck together to make simple structures —such as trains—and these can then be painted, of course.

One is not suggesting that there is anything wrong in making func-

tional toys if children are totally involved in their construction.

But this is not always the case with 'primitive' constructions which simply keep children occupied without demanding any form of decision on their part. The most obvious example of this is when children are told to follow a prescribed pattern or a set of instructions and expected to make something quite specific, which can then be checked as to its perfection and 'correctness'. Such 'creations' are really just another form of paper cut-out and kill children's powers of imagination.

Boxes and tins can be used to lay the table for a lovely birthday party.

Or to make a crossroads with buildings, trees and a fountain.

Not to forget the doll's house.

An exotic aquarium is made out of a shoe-box.

Or a fuel pump out of large cardboard boxes.

Or a car big enough to sit in.

Or buildings large enough to play 'house' in. There is an infinite number of possibilities. What about a really big cardboard house with windows which open and close, and which could even be used as a puppet theatre?

That was an excursion into the field of transforming objects into things to be played with or looked at. They can be painted with casein emulsion colour, water colours, distemper or enamels—or covered with coloured paper. But let us get back to the actual object, the pictorial object, which speaks for itself and does not rely on outside influences for meaning. We can stay with the cardboard box.

The cube offers the opportunity of gaining insight into the relationships between different colours. The interior can be used to illustrate colour combinations.

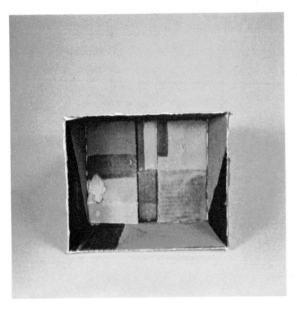

We can use all sorts of free colour arrangements and create a collage, for example.

The construction of a whole wall out of coloured cubes could also be very rewarding. So far we have mainly used the cubes to express various colour combinations; now we can go on to transform them spatially, using colour as an extra dimension.

Up to now we have simply used the interior of the cubes; now we can extend their use. We can create what could be called a 'three-dimensional collage'.

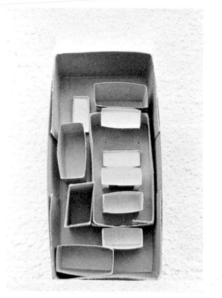

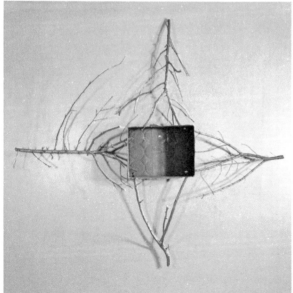

In this way we freely invent and create individual structures with a value of their own. Here space is used to its full measure by means of painted branches. The interior space is 'traversed' in one example and embraced in the other.

It should be stressed that the information offered here is to be taken only as exemplary—it is obviously impossible to mention everything which can be made. The sorts of things which can be created with a cardboard box can also be created with a barrel, a bucket or a tube. Let your imagination run free. It is hoped that the reader will go far beyond the scope of this book and show that the author has omitted to list all sorts of things. In many cases the objects could be more beautiful and more varied. The aim of this book is simply to give some basic guidance.

So far we have only glued and painted the constructions. If the basic material is tin, however, we can also solder, cut and bend the object. This will be more suitable for older children, as the handling of tin-cutting shears requires some amount of strength; the soldering iron should also be used with care and skill.

Tins can be opened and soldered together.

All sorts of constructions can be invented if all the scrap metal to be found is considered according to how it can be used pictorially.

Polystyrene—which is often used in packaging—can also produce interesting effects. It is sometimes found as moulds and prefabricated shapes, and these can be transformed into new objects by cutting, glueing, rearranging and painting.

Polystyrene moulds, with their slits and indentations, can also be filled with smaller objects. These can be left as they are or painted different colours.

Really there is hardly anything that could not become an object of transformation. It could be a brick to which we give a totally new appearance; or a decaying tree trunk which we transform by planing, cutting and drilling it; or a piece of wood which we drill with holes, singe with the soldering iron and treat with a hard brush. (Here chance combines with the object.)

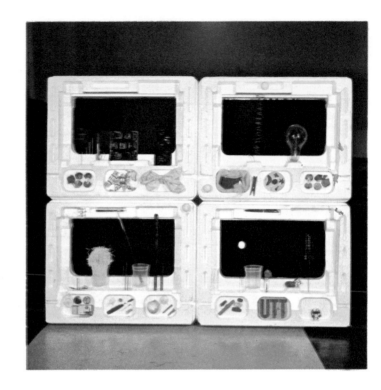

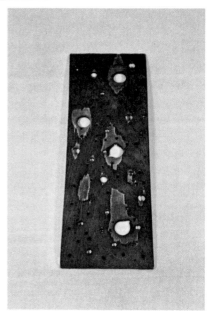

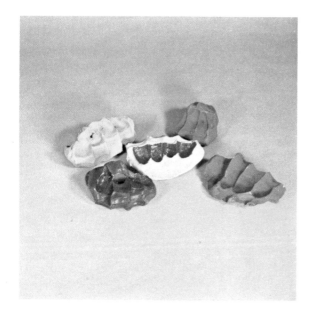

Just as we can transform chance finds in order to produce pictorial objects, we can also 'invent' objects consciously; creations which simply portray themselves.

Objects are three-dimensional structures and their validity is not simply dependent on their purpose.

They are a proof of all the pictorial possibilities open to us. They can become a reality in themselves. The attentive reader will realize that there is a lot more to them even than this.

Further suggestions

For the child the most important form of work is play. While playing, the child develops its knowledge of the world and learns much more than the adult achieves by hard work.

Children deal with objects whose meaning is unknown to them. They take these objects into their world and give them a place there. We adults should show great respect for this, for it would be a good thing if we could approach the phenomena of our world with the same open-mindedness. It is our job to teach children to have a conscious position in the world; but we should not over-train or manipulate them. We must try to make them familiar with those things which we have found by experience to be necessary and viable.

But even more important: we must give them the chance to be inwardly and outwardly prepared and ready to take their own decisions, so that they will be able to exist in a future which is unknown to us all. And existence means more than just not starving. It means an inner and outer existence, a readiness to act; it means possessing self-knowledge, judge-

ment and one's own views. It means having the ability to change the world.

By allowing children to deal with objects and chance we place them in a situation where they are able to make their own decisions. It is a challenging situation, where success and failure are very different from the success and failure involved in a challenge to represent some literary theme pictorially.

Chance and object confront every child in the same way. They provoke creative action; they are ready to be transformed in a thousand different ways. It is part of children's nature to enjoy dealing with and transforming things. Taking this as a starting point, art education can use objects and chance directly to engage children's interest and attention.

The Distribution of Materials
Every teacher should try this method out once, and generally speaking it is not dependent on the age of the children.

All sorts of different items are collected in a sack or large box: tins, sewing reels, wire, small boxes, wood shavings, nails,

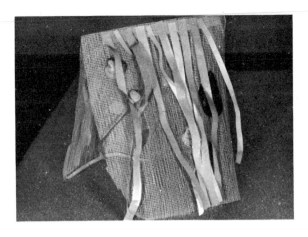

they may well ask. The straight-forward answer is: 'So that you can make something out of it.'

At first the children may be some-what bewildered and perhaps even at a loss. But curiosity will make them pick something out and start experimenting with it. Copying from others is allowed. The author has played the game 'What can you make out of this?' in many classes of different age ranges, and the most amazing and wonderful objects have resulted from it. I have rarely seen children so deeply involved and full of enthusiasm. The children should, of course, also be given glue and adhesives.

screws, twigs, bits of material, old rags, scraps of coloured paper, empty cigarette packets and matchboxes, pieces of string, wooden beads, pieces of poly-styrene, silver paper, etc.

All these 'treasures' are then spread out in front of the class. The children are invited to inspect everything and to help themselves to anything they want. 'Why?'

It is interesting to note that the resulting 'creatures' prompted the strangest descriptions from the children. Banal concepts such as 'beautiful' or 'correct' did not even occur to them.

What does the child get out of it?

This is surely the most important question the teacher should ask himself. In our case the child learns to think with the help of the object. The hands touch it, the eyes test it; long-forgotten ideas are revived. Everything is arranged so that the child produces things on his own. The importance of employing chil-dren's technical skills in using

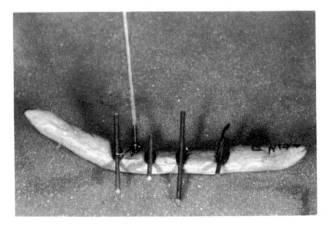

their hands cannot be stressed too strongly.

Dealing with objects picked up by chance is, in a sense, like practising for the 'real event'. All sorts of artistic, graphic, constructive and plastic techniques come into play automatically and out of necessity. The 'real event' for which we are practising is everyday life—adult life—when one must constantly get the hang of things and get things done. For it is characteristic of man not simply to accept matter and tolerate chance, but consciously to transform matter, to explore chance, and to use the acquired knowledge to the advantage of himself and others.

It is hoped that the examples which follow in the Appendix will provide further suggestions for the pictorial use of chance objects.

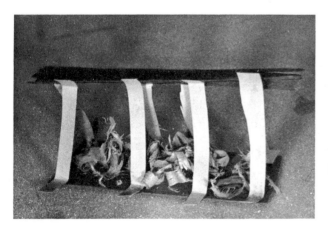
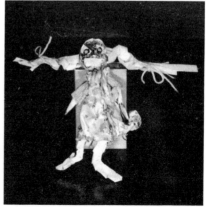

Appendix—examples of pupils' and students' work.

These were supposed to be 'black suns', but too much ink was poured on to the wet paper. The 'spoilt' sheet of paper was put to one side and began to dry at the edges. Then someone had the idea of washing the ink away from the middle of the paper by running water over it. (Boy, aged 10)

The background is formed by a rubbing which had been ruined. Free-flowing drops of enamel gave it a completely new perspective. Touches of water colour completed the picture. (Student)

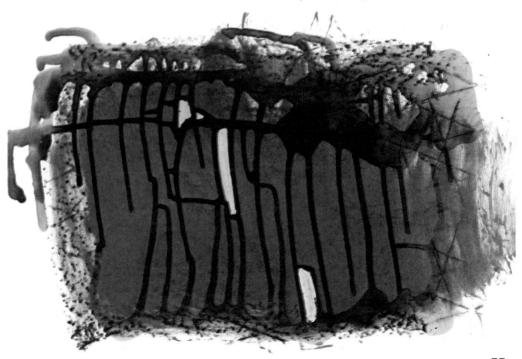

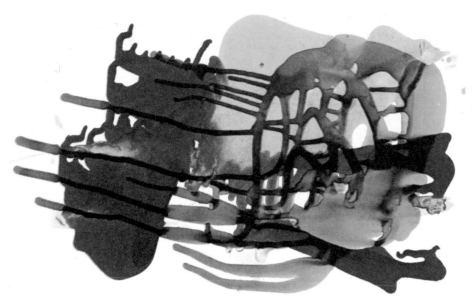

Pools of enamel were the foundation. The paper was then tilted so that the pools ran into each other.

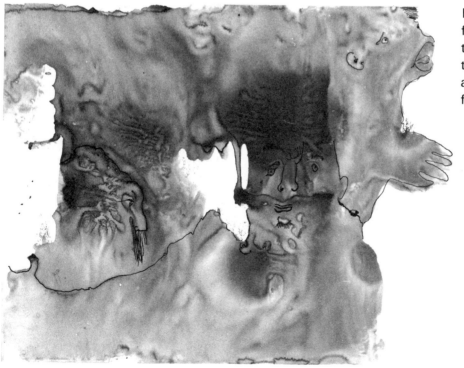

Print taken on paper from a pool of ink on the floor. The features thus obtained were accentuated with a fine nib (Student)

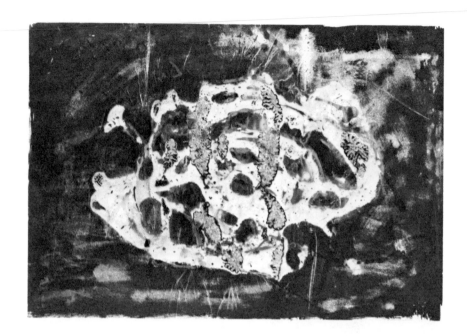

A combination of linseed oil and drawing ink. It took days for the linseed oil to dry. Where it had been applied too thickly it began to look like bark. When it was finally dry, the paper was washed in an ink-soluble solution. (Boy, aged 12)

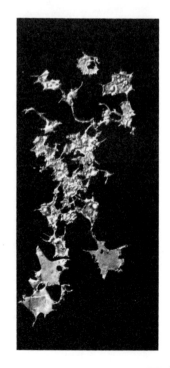

While soldering, drops of liquid tin sometimes drop on the floor; they splash, form bizarre shapes and then dry immediately. They can easily be picked up, re-arranged and then stuck on to a dark background with general-purpose adhesive. (Boy, aged 10)

Bits of wax painting crayon were placed between a folded sheet of paper and then ironed with a hot iron. So this could be called a 'folded print'! (Girl, aged 13)

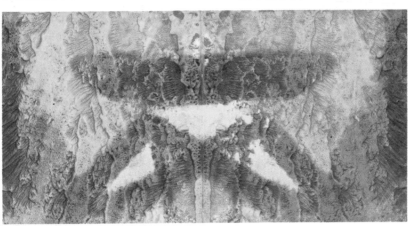

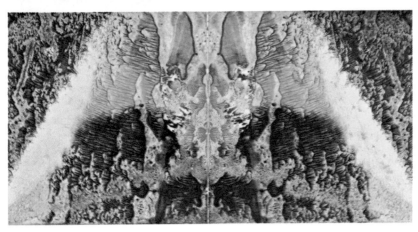

Collage made up of pieces cut out
from random materials. (Girl, aged
12)

Collage of various prints.

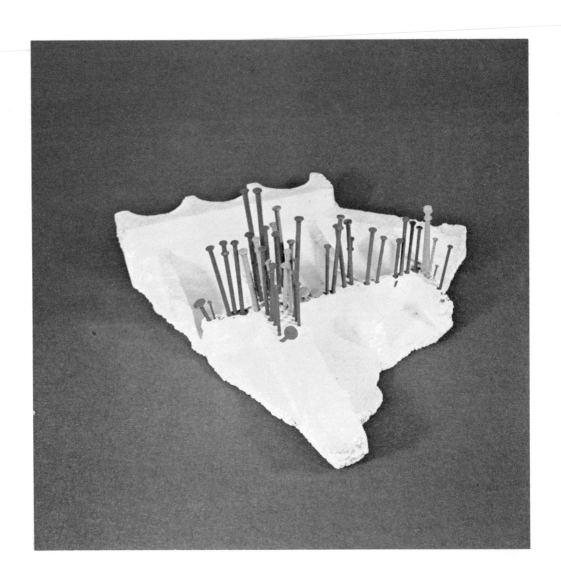

Structure of polystyrene and painted nails. (Girl, aged 11)

Pieces of cardboard, painted and placed one behind the other. (Boy, aged 12)

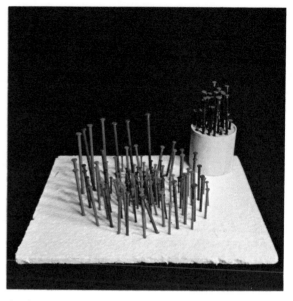

A tin and a board of nails. (Boy, aged 10)

Decorative spatial object made with plastic bottle tops. (Girl, aged 12)

Structures made from cigarette packets and pieces of polystyrene. (Boy, aged 11)

Robots made from cardboard boxes. (Boy, aged 12)

Pieces of polystyrene of various sizes were 'marked' with a nitro-solution, which dissolves the plastic and eats it away. The separate pieces were then arranged as a group. (Boy, aged 11)

'Mass object' made of paper soaked in plaster of Paris, to which stones and other random objects were added.

'Pillar structures'—nails, egg boxes, balls of polystyrene etc.

A piece of cloth was stuck to an old window and touches of casein emulsion added. (Student)

A circuit diagram structure. (Boy, aged 14)

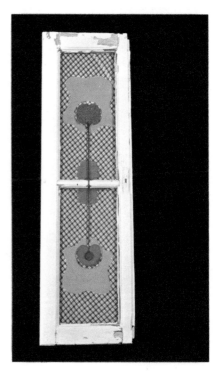

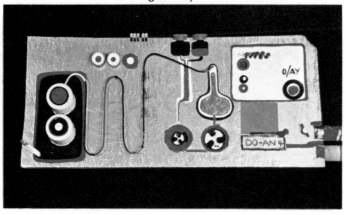

Old shoes and boots were painted.
(Girl and boy, aged 10 and 12)

Branches decorated with buttons.
(Girl, aged 13)

Pieces of bark put together to form
a relief. (Girl, aged 11)

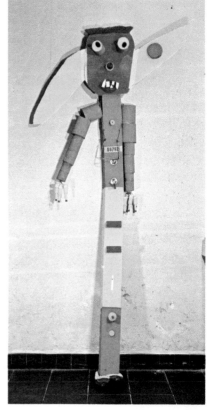

A larger-than-life cardboard figure.
(Boy, aged 12)

Objects made of shells. (Student)

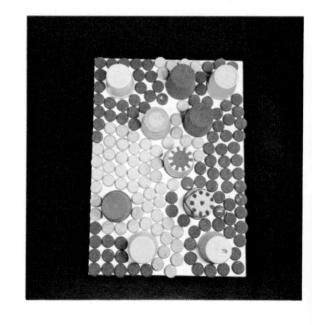

Creations in relief from egg containers, plastic cups and bottle tops. (Boy and girl, aged 12)

Object made of cheese boxes,
gauze and polystyrene.

Table of Technical Skill Levels for Grades 1 through 10

It is hard to tell how old a child has to be in order to associate with objects found by chance. Actually there are no age limits; one can only recommend grades according to the technical difficulties or the children's ability to use the objects. Therefore, the following table is only based on practical experiences in schools. Depending upon the teaching method, the experiences can lead to new approaches at any time.

Grades 1 and 2: 9, 14, 21, 22, 24, 25, 29, 30, 32, 35, 36, 37 top, 38 bottom, 39 top, 40, 41, 44, 50, 51 bottom, 52

Grades 3 and 4: 9, 10, 12, 14, 18, 21, 22, 24, 25, 27, 29, 30, 32, 35, 36, 37 top and bottom, 38 bottom, 39, 40, 41, 42, 44, 49, 50, 51 bottom, 52

Grades 5–7: 9, 10, 11, 12, 14, 15, 16, 17, 18, 19, 20, 21, 22, 23, 24, 25, 26, 27, 28, 29, 30, 31, 32, 33, 34, 35, 36, 37 top and bottom, 38 bottom, 39, 40, 41, 42, 43, 44, 45, 46, 47, 49, 50, 51 bottom, 52

Grades 8–10: 9, 10, 11, 12, 14, 15, 16, 17, 18, 19, 20, 21, 22, 23, 24, 25, 26, 27, 28, 29, 30, 31, 32, 33, 34, 35, 36, 37, 38, 39, 40, 41, 42, 43, 44, 45, 46, 47, 48, 49, 50, 51, 52

Index